OLYMPIC JUDO
groundwork techniques

OLYMPIC JUDO
groundwork techniques

NEIL ADAMS, MBE, and CYRIL A. CARTER

PELHAM BOOKS · LONDON

To Sharon

First published in Great Britain by
Pelham Books Ltd
27 Wrights Lane, Kensington, London W8 5D2
1986

British Library Cataloguing in Publication Data

Adams, Neil
    Olympic judo: groundwork techniques.
    1. Judo
    I. Title   II. Carter, Cyril
    796.8′152   GV1114

ISBN 0 7207 1670 5

Typeset, printed and bound in Great Britain by
Butler & Tanner Limited, Frome and London

Contents

Acknowledgements

Many thanks to Ray Stevens for his magnificent role as Uke in the photographs; we are sure that this experience will allow him to remove the 'L' and 'R' labels from his wrists and ankles sooner than would otherwise have been the case – only joking, Ray!

Thanks also to our respective wives, Alison and Rita, for putting up with silly antics, practical jokes, and general attacks of lunacy that always occur when delinquent judo players are asked to sit down for more than ten minutes at a stretch. Particular thanks to Rita for taking dictation and typing the manuscripts (no, Rita, 'Tori' is not something you shout at a bull!) and for appreciating the cabaret and floor show when we all should have been working.

We also acknowledge the splendid work of our photographer David 'Clicky' Finch, some of whose shots range from the indecent to plain pornographic (if you sell those pictures to the newspapers you can expect a visit from 'the boys'). Thanks too to Charles Palmer for writing the Foreword (who gave you permission to change hats again?) and the British Judo Association for permission to use the material in the Appendix.

We would also like to thank Muriel Gascoin and Ruth Baldwin of Pelham Books (the excuses were genuine, honest!); the Budokwai Judo Club for permission to use their dojo (haven't you guys ever heard of central heating?); and Bob, the dog, for chewing the steering wheel and car upholstery, thus ensuring that the royalties cannot now be spent on something frivolous like food, paying bills, repaying the bank, etc.

Foreword

by CHARLES PALMER, OBE, 8th Dan
President of the British Judo Association
Chairman of the British Olympic Association

There is a plethora of judo books on the market which must, in part, be as a result of the success which Great Britain has achieved in this deeply rewarding sport. More people are taking up judo in this country, either as recreation or as a serious sport, than has ever been the case before and it is no coincidence that this has happened just at the point when one of our number, Neil Adams, has distinguished himself as one of the best judoka the world has ever seen.

Neil Adams, MBE, 5th Dan, double Olympic Silver Medallist, 1981 World Champion and six times European Champion, has combined with his personal coach Cyril Carter to produce two books which examine the two major aspects of judo: Tachi-waza (throwing) and Ne-waza (groundwork). Both are instructional books with a difference in that not only do they examine the 'fundamental' aspects of the major techniques used in contest and randori today, they go uniquely further by outlining the variation and combination of techniques so vital to the judoka who wishes to explore the sheer artistry of judo and who wants to develop a deeper understanding of how techniques are developed, adapted and combined to greater effect.

Neil's technical excellence, together with his vast knowledge of the sport, mean that this book will promote success for all those who study and practise judo and will be of particular use to those who wish to emulate his success by developing a sound repertoire of techniques. Cyril, despite not having Neil's vast judo contest experience, nevertheless brings a valuable critical perspective to the work as a result both of his gymnastic background and his unique coaching relationship with Neil and his predecessor, Brian Jacks. I believe that this book, especially when read with its companion, *Olympic Judo: Throwing Techniques*, will do a great deal to encourage further participation and success in the sport of judo.

Introduction

There are numerous books about judo providing ample coverage of the fundamentals of the sport. In this book and its companion, *Olympic Judo: Throwing Techniques*, we have tried to go one stage further by linking fundamental techniques to several of the variations popularly used in contest judo and then looking at each technique when used in combination with others. By doing this we hope that the reader will get a small taste of the infinite variety of skills available to the modern-day judoka and further appreciate the sheer complexity and artistry that makes our sport exciting both to watch and in which to participate.

It is Neil Adams's ability to adapt and adopt new learning strategies in judo techniques that makes his performance so thrilling and convincing. His six European titles, two Olympic silver medals and World title are merely icing on the cake compared to the respect his style of judo commands internationally. This reputation took many, many years to accrue and I suppose, for the two of us, the road to success seriously began in the build-up to the winning of Neil's first senior title in the All England Championships in 1976, reaching its most exciting peak (to date) in the winning of the World Championships in 1981.

Championships are never, of course, won by technique alone. The physical equivalent of chess – hence the use of the term 'player' – judo similarly demands a high degree of sophistication in the selection of appropriate tactics: considering whether to place oneself in possible danger in an attempt to gain positional advantage, choosing the appropriate moment to execute a technique or deciding to await a better opportunity, balancing possible risk against probable gain, seeking ways in which to exert pressure rather than have to respond to it. Neil's ability to cope with the many facets of the sport makes him stand out as one of the world's finest ever judokas.

It was never our intention, nor could it ever be possible, to write a book which implies that you can be a novice at page 1 and a champion by the time you have completed reading it. Indeed, in order to appreciate this book more fully it is desirable – though not imperative – that the reader should already have basic knowledge, understanding and experience of the sport. For this reason also we have attempted to keep verbal explanation to a minimum, as well as feeling that 'a picture tells a thousand words' and that each individual player will go on to find his own unique method of performance.

Like all good judo players, Neil operates on both the left- and the right-hand side, and the photographs and text thus reflect the particular side upon which Neil prefers to operate the technique displayed. Therefore, to operate any technique on the opposite side to the one shown, simply substitute 'left' for 'right' in the text and vice versa.

It should also be noted that the first attack should always be pressed home unless the desired reaction is achieved which must result automatically in the execution of a well-practised combination technique. Although combination techniques are strategically planned, they should be tactically executed instinctively. In other words, combination techniques (like all individual techniques) should be practised and rehearsed to the point where the player responds without conscious thought to the situation that his opponent presents. Only in this way will the speed of execution be faster than thought and be fully effective.

The combinations described in this book are shown, as is traditionally coached, as a bringing together of two individual techniques. We have described merely those combinations which we feel to have been particularly effective to date, and we are well aware that these represent only a very small proportion of the infinite number of variations and combinations available to the competent judo player. By studying these combinations any player with sufficient artistic and scientific knowledge of the sport can come up with completely original and devastating techniques – that alone would fulfil the intentions of this book. It may well be that future practice will involve the combination of three techniques: such departures from the norm are what makes judo an exciting sport.

We have attempted, where possible, to attribute the techniques covered here to those players or nations who are noted for their performance. We would like to apologise if there have been any omissions or mistakes in doing so.

Whatever else Neil goes on to achieve, nothing will ever match the enjoyment and elation I have experienced when our combined strategies and tactics have come together to produce a championship performance, whether in minor competitions or in the Olympic Games themselves, or even during practice in the dojo. Nothing more, or less, can satisfy the demanding judo player or his coach. We are fortunate to have experienced many such occasions together, and if this book helps you to appreciate our aims, we are more than satisfied that we have contributed to the highest ideals of our sport.

Cyril A. Carter

I JUJI-GATAME
cross armlock

For the basic technique Tori lies at right angles to his opponent with his legs lying across Uke's chest and throat; it is important for Tori to establish firm contact with Uke's shoulder by means of his groin and upper thighs. In this position Tori takes a grip of Uke's wrist with both hands, placing both palms on the inner side of the wrist and the thumbs on the outer side, and extends the arm up towards his chest, maintaining a grip on Uke's upper arm with his thighs.

With Uke's wrist uppermost, Tori lifts his hips to secure the armlock on the elbow of the fully extended arm (Fig 1).

Fig. 1

Fig. 2   Fig. 3   Fig. 4

Variation 1   Rolling Juji-gatame – left arm/left shoulder
(Adams – Great Britain)

With Uke assuming a defensive posture, Tori approaches
from his right side and, controlling him by placing his chest
firmly against his back and upper shoulders, he places his left
leg over Uke's back and inserts it under his abdomen and in
between his bent legs. Tori's aim is to hook his left foot
against Uke's left thigh. Tori then inserts his left arm underneath Uke's left armpit and secures a firm grip on Uke's left
wrist (Fig 2). This procedure can be followed even when
Uke's left arm is slightly extended from his body in order to
maintain balance, although Uke will normally pull the arm
into his body in an attempt to defend against a basic armlock.

Having established a grip on Uke's left wrist, Tori rolls
and falls forward on to his left shoulder (Fig 3), maintaining
the hooking action of his left foot but leaving his right leg
slightly extended and alongside the top of Uke's head.

The next step is for Tori to manoeuvre his right leg under
Uke's head so that the back of his knee is placed firmly against
the side of Uke's face and throat (Fig 4). Using Uke's head as
a lever, Tori rolls over his left shoulder and on to his back
while driving his right leg strongly against Uke's head (Fig 5).
This action results in Uke being pitched quickly over on to
his back ready for Tori to prise his bent left arm into an
extended position in order to operate the Juji-gatame (Fig 6).
Even an extremely strong and defensive judo player will find
it almost impossible to defend against the extension of his
arm if Tori first pulls Uke's forearm upwards towards Uke's
head immediately prior to extending it fully. The armlock is
then operated in the normal manner (Fig 7).

Fig. 5

Fig. 6

Fig. 7

13

Fig. 8

Fig. 9

Fig. 10

Variation 2   Rolling Juji-gatame – right arm/right shoulder
(Yaskovitch – USSR)

Once again with Uke in a defensive posture, Tori straddles
his opponent and hooks his left foot on to Uke's left thigh in
the manner described above (Fig 8). From this position Tori
then inserts his right arm over Uke's left shoulder to hook it
around his opponent's left arm by placing it under either
Uke's left elbow or armpit (Fig 9). Having secured Uke's right
arm, Tori rolls over Uke's head and on to his right side, thus
releasing his hooking left foot which has, up to this point,
been controlling his opponent. Uke's head has now been
forced firmly into the ground, thus raising his seat; maintaining the grip on Uke's right arm, Tori catches hold of the
end of Uke's left trouser leg and commences to pull and draw
this leg in a clockwise direction around and over his own
head (Fig 10). This movement will cause Uke to roll and spin
across Tori's right leg and land on his back with Tori's left
leg across his chest (Fig 11). Tori quickly places his right
leg over Uke's head in order to control Uke's upper body
movement. With his right arm now hooking Uke's left elbow,
Tori commences to secure his grip on Uke's arm and starts
his attempt to extend it fully into the Juji-gatame, in the
manner described above (Fig 12).

Fig. 11

Fig. 12

Variation 3   Spinning Juji-gatame

When Tori is lying on his back, having drawn Uke into a position between his legs (Fig 13), he invites Uke to take a grip on the lapel of his jacket. At that point Tori spins sideways on his back in order to bring his leg around and hook it firmly against the side of Uke's head, simultaneously trapping Uke's arm firmly against his abdomen (Fig 14). Tori's right leg is now in a position at the side of Uke's upper chest. By crossing his legs, Tori achieves firm control of Uke's upper body and, by slipping his arm underneath his body and placing the back of his hand firmly against the knee furthest from him, stops this leg from moving (Fig 15). Tori then drives his legs firmly against Uke's head and shoulders and Uke's blocked knee causes him to pitch sharply over on to his back. From this position Tori swiftly achieves a grip on Uke's arm and extends it upwards and outwards into the Juji-gatame (Fig 16).

Fig. 13

Fig. 14

Fig. 15

Fig. 16

Fig. 17

Fig. 18

Fig. 19

COMBINATION TECHNIQUES

1 Tai-otoshi/Juji-gatame

Having executed the Tai-otoshi (Figs 17 and 18), Tori will quite often find, and should encourage, Uke to roll away from him in order to attempt to escape groundwork (Fig 19). By retaining a firm grip on his opponent's right sleeve, Tori can commence his attack with Juji-gatame. Uke's rolling action, combined with a pull on his right sleeve, extends the right arm into a perfect position for the attack to commence. Simultaneously with securing a firm grip on Uke's right wrist, Tori steps forward on his left foot to place it in front of

Fig. 20   Fig. 21

Uke's head while maintaining firm contact with his right foot
against Uke's back (Fig 20). From this position Tori simply
rolls on to his back and secures a Juji-gatame in the normal
way, although he may choose, as in Fig 21, to leave his right
foot under Uke's back so that it acts as a wedge to prevent
him turning towards him.

2 Sankaku-jime/Juji-gatame

With Uke positioned between his legs (Fig 22), Tori takes a firm grip on Uke's right upper sleeve and, at the same time as pulling on this sleeve, he spins on his back, rotating his right leg around and over Uke in order to place the back of his right knee firmly against the side of Uke's neck (Figs 23 and 24). Using this leg as a lever against Uke's head, Tori maintains the pulling action on Uke's sleeve in order to draw his right shoulder downwards towards the ground (Fig 25). As Uke is forced downwards, Tori quickly traps his right wrist with his left hand, simultaneously taking his right leg over to hook the back of his calf against the hooking instep of his left foot. The Sankaku-jime is now locked firmly into place, but where Uke's right arm has not been securely forced against the side of his neck to operate the strangle, Tori continues to rotate, while rolling Uke firmly over on to his back (Fig 26) and maintaining his grip on Uke's right wrist.

Fig. 22

Fig. 23

Fig. 24

Fig. 25

Uke's right arm is now available for the operation of Juji-gatame and, should he defend, may be fully extended in the manner described above (Fig 27).

Fig. 26   Fig. 27

Fig. 28

3 Kesure-kesa-gatame/Juji-gatame

Having secured Kesure-kesa-gatame, but in such a way that there is a risk of Uke's escaping from this position (Fig 28), Tori can change swiftly into an attack for an immediate submission with Juji-gatame. Maintaining a secure trapping action on Uke's right arm, Tori quickly raises himself into a kneeling position on his right knee and rotates his left leg around Uke's head so that he is straddling Uke's upper body (Fig 29). Tori swiftly secures a grip on Uke's jacket with his right hand and sits back sharply in order to trap Uke's right wrist under his left armpit (Fig 30). With his left leg controlling Uke's head and his right foot controlling Uke's back, Tori simply lies back and lifts his hips to apply the Juji-gatame (Fig 31).

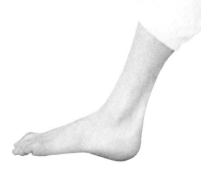

Fig. 29

Fig. 30

Fig. 31

II SANKAKU-JIME
three-cornered or triangular strangle

With Uke positioned between his legs, Tori takes a firm grip on Uke's right upper sleeve and, at the same time as pulling on this sleeve, he spins on his back rotating his right leg around and over Uke in order to place the back of his right knee firmly against the side of Uke's neck (Fig 32). Using this leg as a lever against Uke's head, Tori maintains the pulling action on Uke's sleeve in order to draw his right shoulder downwards towards the ground (Fig 33). As Uke is forced downwards, Tori quickly traps his right wrist with his left hand, simultaneously taking his right leg over to hook the back of his calf against the hooking instep of his left foot (Fig 34). The Sankaku-jime is now locked firmly into place with Uke's right arm being securely forced against the side of his own neck to operate the strangle.

Fig. 32

Fig. 33

24

Fig. 34

Variation 1   Sankaku-jime – rolling sideways (Gilbert – France)

With Uke adopting a defensive posture, Tori approaches from his left side and places his left arm under Uke's left armpit to secure a grip on Uke's left wrist (Fig 35). Tori then pulls this wrist upwards to trap it firmly against Uke's chest (Fig 36) and proceeds to pivot, with his chest against Uke's back, to rotate his left leg around Uke's head and hook it through the space between Uke's right arm and right knee (Figs 37 and 38). This action results in Tori sitting on Uke's head and forcing it down towards the mat. Tori now drives his left foot through and underneath Uke's body, while continuing to pull Uke's left arm upwards and over, simultaneously dropping on to his left side and back (Fig 39).

Fig. 35

Fig. 36

Fig. 37

Fig. 38

Fig. 39

Fig. 40

Uke has now been forced to rotate on to his back and Tori brings his right leg up and over Uke's head to hook his heel under Uke's right armpit. With his right arm, Tori reaches over and takes hold of a strap of Uke's belt (or one of the tails of his jacket) and wraps this over Uke's wrist in order to secure the arm fully (Fig 40).

With Uke's left arm now out of action, Tori secures a grip on the sleeve of Uke's right arm and pulls the right upper forearm firmly across and towards Uke's neck. By bending his right leg against this trapped arm, Tori can hook his right foot under the calf of his left leg which is now acting as a pillow for Uke's head and neck. The strangle is operated by squeezing with the legs and with Tori rotating his hips towards Uke's head (Fig 41).

Fig. 41

Fig. 42

Fig. 43

Fig. 44

Fig. 45

Fig. 46

Variation 2   Sankaku-jime – rolling forwards (Adams – Great Britain)

The entry into this variation is exactly the same as described above (Figs 42 and 43) except that, at the point where Tori has inserted his left leg into the space between Uke's right arm and knee, Uke has attempted to sit up by lifting his head and bracing his right arm (Fig 44). Tori then switches the direction of his attack by rolling forwards across Uke's back and on to his left shoulder (Fig 45), simultaneously hooking his left foot under Uke's right arm and using this foot and his right leg braced against Uke's head to rotate Uke upwards and over on to his back (Fig 46).

With Uke now on his back, Tori uncrosses his legs and,

Fig. 47

Fig. 48

by placing his right calf against the outer side of Uke's right elbow, forces this arm up against the side of Uke's neck (Fig 47). This action may also be assisted by Tori securing a grip on the end of Uke's right sleeve and pulling the arm towards him (Fig 48). Uke's left arm can now be secured by trapping it against his chest, using either his belt or the tail of his jacket. The technique is completed when Tori hooks his right instep under the calf of his left leg and leans backwards and over towards Uke's head to operate the strangle.

Fig. 49

Fig. 50

Fig. 51

Fig. 52

Fig. 53

Fig. 54

Variation 3   Sankaku-jime – turn-over (Van der Walle – Belgium)

Approaching his opponent from the front, Tori takes hold of Uke's belt and inserts his left foot into the space between Uke's right knee and arm (Fig 49). Tori then takes a firm grip on Uke's left sleeve and pulls that arm around and upwards, simultaneously sliding his left leg underneath Uke's body (Fig 50). This causes Tori to pivot on to his left side and back so that his right buttock and leg are controlling Uke's head (Fig 51).

Uke has now been forced to rotate over his right side and on to his back. Tori proceeds to 'tie his parcel' by securing Uke's left arm using either his belt or the tail of his jacket (Fig 52). With his opponent now secure, Tori reaches across and takes hold of Uke's right sleeve in order to force that arm securely against Uke's neck (Fig 53). The strangle is completed by Tori hooking his right instep under his left calf (Fig 54).

Fig. 55

Fig. 56

Fig. 57

32

COMBINATION TECHNIQUES

1 Juji-gatame/Sankaku-jime – sitting up

With Tori attacking Uke's right arm for a Juji-gatame submission and his opponent strongly defending, Tori creates a space between Uke's arms and chest by pulling vigorously and painfully against the inside of Uke's elbow (Fig 55). Having created a gap, Tori inserts his right leg through this opening and places it across Uke's throat and upper chest (Fig 56). Maintaining his pulling action as if he were still pursuing the Juji-gatame (Fig 57), he removes his left foot which, up until now, has been controlling Uke's head; this results in Uke attempting to sit up forwards. Tori completes the Sankaku-jime by placing his right leg into the space created between Uke's head and the floor and locks his right instep under his left calf (Fig 58). The strangle is then operated in the normal manner.

Fig. 58

33

Fig. 59

Fig. 60

Fig. 61

2 Juji-gatame/Sankaku-jime – arching

With Tori attacking Uke's left arm for Juji-gatame, and with his opponent once again strongly defending (Fig 59), Tori creates space between Uke's arm and chest in exactly the same manner as for the first combination (Fig 60). This time he changes the direction of his attack by inserting his right leg through the space provided and takes his left leg away from Uke's chest and places his foot under Uke's left side (Fig 61).

By pulling strongly on Uke's left arm, Tori encourages Uke to arch and roll towards him in order to escape the pain of the attack on his arm (Fig 62). Tori seizes this opportunity to insert his left leg under Uke's back and place it in a position

Fig. 62

Fig. 63

to act as a 'pillow' for Uke's head. He then 'ties up' Uke's left arm either by using the belt or tail of the jacket or by applying a figure 4 armlock on Uke's wrist and forearm. Tori next wraps his right leg firmly around and against Uke's right upper arm, thus trapping it against the side of Uke's neck. The strangle is completed by Tori locking his right instep against his left calf (Fig 63).

III KAMI-SHIHO-GATAME
upper four-quarters hold-down

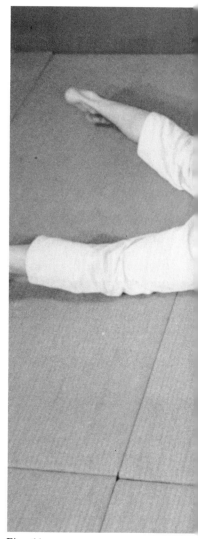

Fig. 64

Approaching Uke over his left shoulder, Tori traps this shoulder and his opponent's chest by lying so that his belt-line is next to Uke's head. Tori then places his arms underneath Uke's arms and takes a firm grip on his belt at either side of his body. By exerting downward pressure with his chest and head, and by squeezing his arms tightly against Uke's upper arms, Tori pins Uke firmly to the floor (Fig 64).

Tori's legs are normally spread straight and wide apart and the balls of his feet remain in firm contact with the ground to avoid the danger of being rolled to either side.

It is important to point out at this stage that, although these hold-downs are regarded as being more secure when Tori straightens his legs and maintains firm contact with his opponent, experience has shown that, especially with a stronger opponent, it is often more desirable to avoid too firm a body contact as this enables the stronger man to apply his force more efficiently. By kneeling up and creating a little space, Tori has time to anticipate his opponent's attempted movements and can then cushion and suppress them more efficiently and effectively.

Variation 1   Kame-shiho-gatame – bent legs

Tori may choose to vary the technique by bending both legs so that his knees are now in firm contact with the ground (Fig 65). Although as a result he is in some danger of being rolled sideways by a stronger opponent, Tori is in a much better position to move quickly to seize a variety of alternatives which are now open to him: another hold-down or possibly a strangle or an armlock.

Fig. 65

Fig. 66

Variation 2   Kuzure-kame-shiho-gatame – broken upper four-quarters hold-down

In this variation Tori has relinquished the hold of one of his hands on Uke's belt and has wrapped that 'free' arm firmly under and around Uke's neck (Fig 66). This action provides a firmer control of Uke's head in order to ensure that he is locked into the mat.

Fig. 67

Variation 3 Kuzure-kame-shiho-gatame – trapping arm and head

In this variation Tori has taken his right arm over and across Uke's head, right shoulder and chest, and secured a grip on Uke's belt (Fig 67). This action has caused Uke to be firmly pinned by his right shoulder and head. Tori has released his hold on Uke's belt with his left hand and has moved it over his opponent's body to take up a grip on the top of Uke's trouser leg; this helps to prevent Uke from using his legs efficiently in an attempt to escape. Tori may, of course, choose to leave his left arm in the conventional position under Uke's shoulder, and which variation is more comfortable and more successful will depend upon his own upper-arm strength and body control.

COMBINATION TECHNIQUES

1 Front turn-over into Kuzure-kami-shiho-gatame
(Kashiwazake – Japan)

With Uke adopting a defensive posture, Tori approaches him from the front and pushes his right hip firmly against his opponent's right shoulder, simultaneously placing his right arm over Uke's back and securing an overhand grip on his belt (Fig 68). Then, having pulled Uke upwards and forwards in order to create space, Tori inserts his left arm under Uke's right armpit and hooks it around the upper arm (Fig 69).

Next, Tori lifts upwards on Uke's trapped right arm and inserts his right leg under his opponent's body to place it between his bent legs, simultaneously dropping his right hand and forearm across Uke's shoulders (Fig 70). Tori now commences to turn his opponent by lifting upwards on the trapped right arm and exerting contra-rotation by pulling downwards and around on Uke's belt. Once Uke has started to twist, Tori inserts his right leg deeper underneath Uke, drops on to his right side and, using his right leg to lift Uke's lower body, swiftly rotates him over on to his back (Fig 71).

The hold is secured when Tori takes his left arm across Uke's chest and wraps it around and under his opponent's left armpit to secure a grip on the back of his jacket; Tori's right arm maintains a grip on Uke's belt and, by his squeezing tightly with the upper arm, controls his opponent's head (Figs 72 and 73).

Fig. 71

Fig. 68

Fig. 69

Fig. 70

Fig. 72

Fig. 73

2 Rear turn-over into Kuzure-kami-shiho-gatame

Approaching Uke from behind, Tori places both arms under his opponent's armpits and secures a grip on each of the lapels of Uke's jacket, simultaneously hooking his right leg in and around Uke's right knee (Fig 74). Controlling Uke with his trapped right leg, Tori pushes with his free left leg and rotates on to his right side, pulling Uke with him and maintaining his grip on both of the latter's lapels (Fig 75).

With Tori now on his right side, and not 'trapped' on his back, Uke is positioned over Tori's right shoulder (Fig 76). Tori now slides his opponent off his shoulder and, pivoting with his hips, swings both legs out and around so that he eventually pivots around Uke's trapped shoulders to bring his own left shoulder into contact with the back of Uke's head; meanwhile his own head rotates over Uke's right shoulder and Tori traps it with his chin (Figs 77 and 78). Uke is now trapped firmly into the hold-down by Tori's shoulders and chest. Tori may bend both legs so that he is kneeling or, alternatively, may straighten both legs out and press his hips downward into the mat.

Fig. 75

Fig. 74

Fig. 76

Fig. 77

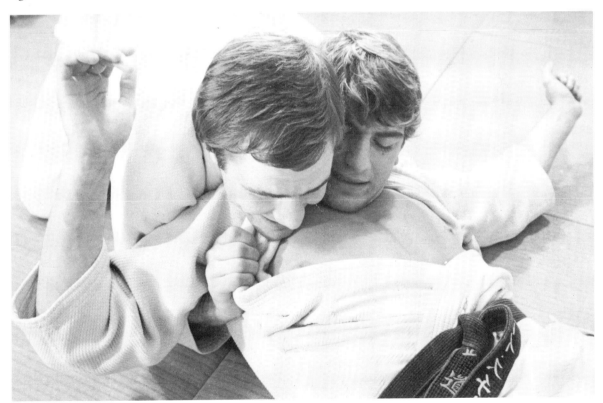

Fig. 78

IV TATE-SHIHO-GATAME
cross-body hold

Tori sits astride his opponent, high up on the abdomen, with both knees in contact with the mat. He then forces Uke's right arm firmly across and against the side of his neck and face, while inserting his own right arm under Uke's neck, so that his upper arm makes firm contact with the side of the neck, and takes a firm grip on the right side of Uke's jacket. Tori then places the side of his head firmly against Uke's bent upper arm in order to trap it firmly into place (Fig 79). With his opponent locked into position, Tori can use his left arm as a stabiliser; or he may choose to use his legs as stabilisers, moving them outward from Uke's body to counteract any twisting movement; or he may cross his feet together under Uke's body to lock him firmly into place. Whichever alternative Tori chooses will depend on the size and nature of Uke and his own preference in terms of comfort and security.

Fig. 79

Variation 1 Rolling Kuzure-tate-shiho-gatame – broken cross-body hold using the leg

The movement begins with Uke on top of Tori and between his legs. Tori's first task is to take his right arm over Uke's left shoulder to secure a firm grip on Uke's belt, pulling his opponent forward to ensure that his left arm is trapped securely between both chests (Fig 80). With Uke's arm trapped, Tori reaches down with his left arm and hooks it underneath and around Uke's right leg. Tori now commences to roll his opponent by lifting his leg and pulling on his belt (Fig 81), thus forcing Uke to pivot over his left shoulder.

As Uke is forced to roll (Fig 82), Tori, keeping his legs straddling his opponent, releases his left arm from under Uke's right leg and is left with several options in order to secure the technique, each depending upon Uke's reactions. Maintaining his grip on Uke's belt, Tori's prime task is to achieve total control of his opponent's head. This he may do by simply placing his own head firmly against his opponent's, while leaving his left arm free to be placed sideways on the floor as a stabiliser or, alternatively, to be slipped under Uke's shoulder and back to secure his opponent's upper body. If Uke's right arm becomes suitably available at the point when the roll is completed and Tori is freeing his own left arm, Tori can swiftly take hold of his opponent's arm and force it against his neck in order to secure a more conventional form of the technique, using his own head then to trap this arm firmly into place.

Fig. 80

Fig. 81

Fig. 82

Fig. 83

Fig. 84

Fig. 85

Variation 2 Rolling Kezure-tate-shiho-gatame using the arm

With Uke attacking Tori from above, Tori forces his opponent down by reaching over his right shoulder and securing a grip on his belt. Pulling sharply on Uke's belt, Tori forces his head on to the mat at a point just under his own right shoulder and traps his opponent's head with his upper arm; this action forces Uke to put his left arm out in order to avoid being rolled to the left (Fig 83). Maintaining the pressure on Uke's head with his upper arm, Tori releases his grip on the belt and slips his right forearm through and under Uke's left upper arm and shoulder (Fig 84).

Using Uke's trapped left shoulder and his own right leg as levers, Tori rolls his opponent sharply in the opposite direction and on to his back, ensuring that both knees are still straddling the waist (Fig 85). Rotating his right forearm and still maintaining control of his opponent's head, Tori secures a strong hold by reaching down and securing a grip on the side of his own belt (Fig 86).

Fig. 86

Fig. 87

Fig. 88

COMBINATION TECHNIQUES

1 Tomoenage/Tate-shiho-gatame

This is possibly one of the most natural combination techniques in judo in that the hold-down seems to follow almost automatically from the movement of the throw, providing Tori remembers to keep a firm grip on his opponent's jacket. Having executed a standard Tomoenage and despite whatever score is achieved (Fig 87), Tori simply continues his backward movement rolling over one shoulder, and opens his legs in order to end up straddling his opponent (Fig 88). Relinquishing his grip on Uke's jacket, Tori can choose either to grip for a Kuzure (broken) hold-down or may trap Uke's arm firmly against his own neck for a standard Tate-shiho-gatame. His choice will depend upon Uke's reaction and his own preference (Fig 89).

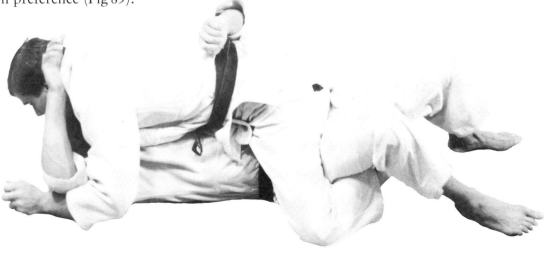

Fig. 89

Fig. 90

Fig. 91

Fig. 92

2 Sumigaeshi-tate-shiho-gatame

This combination is performed in a similar manner to the one involving Tomoenage except that the hooking action of the foot against the inside of Uke's thigh assists in maintaining control of the opponent's body when in flight, thus helping to ensure much closer body contact throughout the rolling action and into the hold-down (Figs 90, 91, 92, 93 and 94). Once again Tori may choose to operate the conventional Tate-shiho-gatame or adopt a Kuzure variation.

Fig. 93

Fig. 94

Fig. 95

Fig. 96
50

3 Ushiro-kesa-gatame/Kuzure-tate-shiho-gatame
(Kashiwazake – Japan)

Tori first achieves a Ushiro-kesa-gatame hold-down, where he has trapped Uke's right arm by placing his own right arm under his opponent's right shoulder and securing a grip on Uke's belt (Fig 95). From this position Tori may now choose to control his opponent's frantic efforts to escape, usually by attempting to bridge simply by throwing his left leg and hip across and over his opponent's body (Fig 96) and rotating on to Uke's chest to place his head firmly down and against the side of Uke's right arm (Fig 97). Uke is now pinned securely on his right upper chest and shoulder (Fig 98), and any progress he might make towards an escape by sitting up and rotating may easily be countered by Tori reversing his own movements into Ushiro-kesa-gatame.

Fig. 97

Fig. 98

V YOKO-SHIHO-GATAME
side four-quarters hold

Approaching Uke from his left side, Tori lies at right angles across him, ensuring firm chest-to-chest contact. He places his right forearm underneath his opponent's neck and takes a firm grip high up on the collar, thus controlling the head and preventing Uke from bridging effectively. Tori's left arm is placed firmly under Uke's crotch and he takes a grip high up on his opponent's trousers or his belt. With his legs spread and hips forced downwards for increased stability, Tori locks himself against his opponent's body by squeezing tight with both arms, thus pinning Uke firmly on his back (Fig 99).

Fig. 99

Fig. 100

Variation 1   Yoko-shiho-gatame – kneeling

As with all Kuzure (broken) techniques, there are thousands of minor variations, but three are particularly worthy of mention in the case of Yoko-shiho-gatame.

The first variation, although relatively simple, opens up a myriad of possibilities. Instead of lying flat, Tori kneels up firmly against Uke's left side (Fig 100). The immediate advantage of adopting this position is that Uke is prevented from turning towards his opponent to attempt an escape. Tori, however, by maintaining firm chest contact with his opponent, is in a better position to take advantage of any opportunities that Uke's movements might present to change the form of his hold-down. He may even seek an armlock or strangle simply by breaking his hand-holds and spinning clockwise or anti-clockwise around Uke's chest.

Variation 2   Kuzure-yoko-shiho-gatame – trapping right shoulder

In this variation Tori has elected to kneel firmly up against his opponent's left side so that his chest contacts the right side of Uke's chest. His right arm now goes under his opponent's right shoulder so that, by gripping Uke's belt, that shoulder and arm are firmly trapped in place (Fig 101). With Tori's left arm gripping in the same manner as for the basic technique, the advantage of this particular variation is that there is an open opportunity to change to Ushiro-kesa-gatame should the need arise; also Uke's right arm can be attacked with Ude-garami.

Fig. 101

Fig. 102

Variation 3   Kuzure-yoko – trapping the right arm

The third variation develops directly from the basic technique when Uke either attempts to attack Tori's hold by using his right hand to push against his chin, or tries to roll towards Tori, in an effort to escape, usually throwing his right arm across his own face. In either case Tori quickly seizes the opportunity to take his right arm from underneath his opponent's head, manoeuvre it around the back of Uke's upper arm and, trapping it under his right shoulder, regain his grip under Uke's neck (Fig 102). Once secured, this is a particularly powerful hold-down.

Fig. 103

Fig. 104

Fig. 105

Fig. 106

56

COMBINATION TECHNIQUES

1 Blocking Kosoto-gake/Russian reverse/Yoko-shiho-gatame (Surov – USSR)

Tori first establishes a grip on the back of Uke's left shoulder (Fig 103) with his right hand and, by pulling, forces him to step forward on his left foot. Attacking his opponent's left leg with Kosoto-gake (Fig 104), Tori causes Uke to attempt to shift his weight back, around and on to his right foot. As Uke pulls back, Tori steps forward with his right foot, simultaneously pulling upwards on Uke's right sleeve and slipping his head under Uke's armpit, also increasing the pull on the back of Uke's jacket (Fig 105).

Tori now starts to execute a movement which can only be described as a 'Russian reverse', simply because there is no Japanese term for the move and the first judoka observed executing it in Europe came from the USSR. Tori drives his left foot diagonally sideways almost as if he were attempting to perform the 'splits' (Fig 106) and twists his own hips to the right, simultaneously pulling down and around to the right with the hand gripping the back of Uke's jacket, thus causing his opponent to pitch sharply forward and around Tori's blocking right leg. Continuing to pull and rotate Uke, Tori falls on to his right side (Fig 107) and releases his grip on Uke's left sleeve. Rotating on to his front, Tori secures Yoko-shiho-gatame by thrusting his left arm underneath Uke's crotch to take a firm grip on his opponent's trousers or belt (Fig 108).

Fig. 107

Fig. 108

Fig. 109

Fig. 110

Fig. 111

Fig. 112

2 Yoko-shiho-gatame – backward turn-over
(Gawthorpe – Great Britain)

With Uke attacking from above, Tori twists to his left and
drives his bent right leg underneath his opponent's body to
make firm contact with Uke's abdomen (Fig 109), simultaneously hooking his right foot against Uke's upper thigh
or side (Fig 110). Reaching over his opponent's left shoulder,
Tori secures a firm grip on Uke's belt and draws him forward
and down towards his left shoulder (Fig 111). By swiftly
straightening his right leg, Tori forces Uke to flatten out
(Fig 112) into a position where he is now vulnerable to be
turned. Pulling strongly on Uke's belt and simultaneously
twisting towards his own right side, Tori turns Uke around
and over his right shoulder and on to his back (Fig 113). Tori
can choose to assist the movement by taking a grip on the
bottom of Uke's right trouser leg with his left hand, and he
is now in a perfect position to place his left arm under Uke's
crotch to secure Yoko-shiho-gatame.

Fig. 113

Fig. 114

Fig. 115

Fig. 116

Fig. 117

Fig. 118

Fig. 119

3   Kuzure-yoko-shiho-gatame – side turn-over
(Kashiwazake – Japan)

With Uke attacking from the top, Tori manoeuvres his body slightly to the left in order to insert his right leg between Uke's knees, simultaneously reaching over his opponent's right shoulder with his right arm and inserting his left arm under Uke's right armpit to take a firm hold on Uke's belt with both hands (Fig 114). These manoeuvres may be performed in any order so long as the end result is as described: whether it is more appropriate to achieve the leg position first or the grip on Uke's belt will depend on the latter's movements.

Trapping Uke's head with his right upper arm and forcing it down towards the mat, Tori hooks his right heel behind Uke's knee and, using this leg and his opponent's own right arm as levers, he places his left leg out to the side so that this propping foot can help him start to turn his opponent (Fig 115). The combined action of Tori's left foot and right arm forces Uke to turn on to his right side, at which point he will usually trap Tori's leg between his own legs (Fig 116). Ignoring his trapped right leg, Tori continues the turn and traps Uke's left shoulder and head against the mat (Fig 117).

With Uke trapped underneath him, Tori now turns his attention to releasing his trapped right leg. Using his left hand, Tori takes a firm grip on his opponent's right trouser leg and places his left foot firmly on top of Uke's left knee (Fig 118). The combined action of pulling upwards on Uke's right trouser leg and forcing his left leg out straight breaks Uke's hold and enables Tori to free his trapped right leg (Fig 119). Turning swiftly around and on to his front, Tori can now operate Kuzure-yoko-shiho-gatame (Fig 120).

Fig. 120

Fig. 121

Fig. 122

Fig. 123

4 Okuri-ashi-harai/Yoko-shiho-gatame – sweeping ankle throw

Okuri-ashi-harai is performed when both Uke and Tori are moving sideways. Although this is a common movement in contest or randori (free practice), Tori must encourage his opponent to take an extended step sideways to ensure the successful operation of the technique.

With Uke moving to his right and Tori moving to his left, using an orthodox right-hand grip (Fig 121), Tori plants his left leg on the mat and, just at the point where Uke is closing his left leg towards his right, swiftly sweeps his opponent's left leg in the direction in which it is moving (normally sideways) by placing the sole of his right foot firmly against

Fig. 124

Fig. 125

Uke's left ankle. Simultaneously he lifts upwards on Uke's right sleeve to break his balance and pulls downwards on his left lapel to emphasise the rotation of his opponent's body and trap his left arm (Fig 122), causing Uke to be thrown at right angles to Tori's feet (Fig 123). Fig 124 clearly illustrates Uke's landing position in relation to Tori, and the fact that Tori has full control of Uke's left arm and lapel, though it should be pointed out that Tori would, at this point, be moving extremely swiftly to take up the option of ground-work and to operate Yoko-shiho-gatame (Fig 125).

VI UDE-GARAMI
entangled armlock

For the basic technique Uke lies flat on his back and Tori approaches from the right side and leans across his chest. Tori then takes a firm grip on the inside of Uke's left wrist and bends this arm upwards into a 90-degree angle, palm upwards. He then slips his right hand underneath Uke's elbow and takes a firm hold of his own left wrist (Fig 126). Tori places his right knee against Uke's right side to maintain control and extends his left leg to maintain stability. He may choose to enhance his control of Uke's upper body and head by lying firmly on top of him. From this position the armlock is operated by Tori curling his left hand into the mat and raising his right elbow and wrist, thus creating extreme pressure on Uke's left elbow.

Fig. 126

Fig. 128

Fig. 127

Fig. 129

Variation 1   Sankaku turn into Ude-garami

With Uke adopting a defensive posture, Tori approaches
from his left side and inserts his left arm under Uke's left
armpit to take a firm grip on his opponent's left wrist
(Fig 127). Pulling this wrist sharply down towards Uke's belt-
line, Tori pivots on his right knee (Fig 128), swinging his left
leg over Uke's back and inserting it in the space between
Uke's right knee and upper arm (Fig 129). As Tori performs
this action he releases his grip on Uke's wrist and rotates his
arm so that the back of the hand is firmly hooking Uke's
trapped wrist. He forces Uke on to his back by pivoting over
on to his left side as if going for a Sankaku-jime (see Chapter
II), taking Uke's left arm firmly with him (Fig 130 overleaf).

Fig. 131   Fig. 130

Variation 1 (cont.)

Once on to his side, Tori secures Uke's left arm by gripping his opponent's wrist with his right hand and taking a grip on his own right wrist with his left hand. From this position Tori rolls over so that his abdomen now controls Uke's head and upper chest, and takes Uke's bent left arm outwards away from his side. The armlock is then applied when Tori presses down with his right hand and lifts his left forearm (Fig 131).

Variation 2   Reverse Ude-garami

With Uke attempting to attack Tori from above, Tori encourages his opponent to take a grip with his right hand on the left lapel of his jacket (Fig 132). Tori first takes hold of Uke's right wrist and breaks the grip on his lapel by pushing the arm downwards and outwards towards Uke's belt-line. He then places his right foot against Uke's left knee and simultaneously forces his opponent's left leg straight and lifts strongly on Uke's right arm, forcing him to collapse into a straight body position against Tori's abdomen (Fig 133). Immediately following this, Tori rolls slightly on to his left side and takes his right arm up and over Uke's right shoulder, inserting his right hand under his opponent's right armpit to secure a firm grip on his own left wrist. The armlock is applied when Tori moves strongly towards his right side and applies upward pressure on Uke's elbow (Fig 134).

Fig. 133

Fig. 132

Fig. 134

Fig. 136

Fig. 135

COMBINATION TECHNIQUES

1 Kesure-kesa-gatame/Ude-garami

Having achieved the operation of Kesa-gatame, Tori may choose to go for an immediate submission by changing to Ude-garami. He first releases Uke's right arm which, up until now, has been trapped under his own left armpit (Fig 135). He allows this arm to escape but controls it in such a way that he can achieve a grip on Uke's right wrist. Having achieved this grip, Tori presses downwards on Uke's straight right arm, which is being 'pillowed' by his right thigh (Fig 136). His action causes Uke to bend his arm upwards

68

Fig. 137

Fig. 138

into an angle in order to escape the pain being inflicted on his elbow. Immediately Uke bends his arm, Tori maintains his downward pressure in order to force the back of Uke's hand into the mat (Fig 137). At this point Tori bends his right leg and traps Uke's arm into position. The armlock is then operated by Tori rotating his hips over and towards Uke's head (Fig 138).

Fig. 139

Fig. 140

Fig. 142

2 Ushiro-kesa-gatame/Ude-garami

Having secured Uke with Ushiro-kesa-gatame (reverse scarf hold), Tori will normally attempt to immobilise Uke's free arm, often by pulling it in towards his body and tying it up with his own belt or the tail of his jacket (Fig 139). In order to do this Tori slips his arm under Uke's armpit and upper arm and takes a grip on the upper part of Uke's wrist (Fig 140). Uke's usual reaction is to attempt to pull his arm outwards, away from his body, to prevent Tori from securing this arm (Fig 141). Immediately Tori then places his other hand on top of Uke's wrist and lifts his opponent towards him by pulling upwards on the back of Uke's shoulder (Fig 142). The armlock is completed when Tori presses downwards and backwards against Uke's forearm.

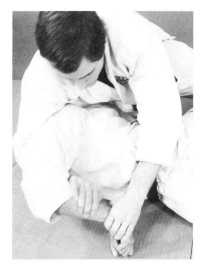

Fig. 141

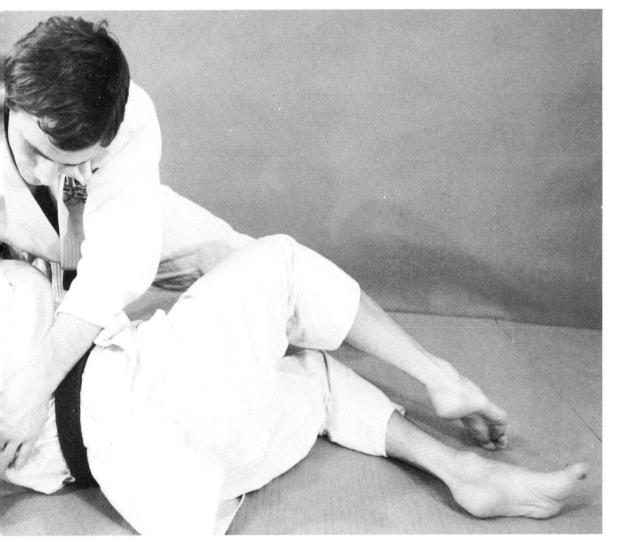

3 Tate-shiho-gatame/Ude-garami

Having secured the Tate-shiho-gatame, where Uke's arm is trapped securely above his own head, Tori can proceed to dispose of his opposition by switching his attention to the Ude-garami (Fig 143). In order to do this he must first take hold of Uke's wrist and pull it in towards the top of Uke's head so that the trapped arm is now severely bent (Fig 144). At this point it is Tori's arm and shoulder that are preventing the movement of Uke's bent elbow and, if Tori replaces this arm by positioning his head against the side of Uke's elbow, he now frees both arms for the operation of Ude-garami. Taking hold of Uke's wrist with both hands, Tori pulls outwards and away from his head while operating a contrary force with his head against Uke's elbow (Fig 145). The lock is now fully operated.

Fig. 143

Fig. 144

Fig. 145

73

4 Juji-gatame/Ude-garami (Seisenbacker – Austria)

With Tori attempting to execute a Juji-gatame roll (see Chapter I), it often happens that the pressure exerted on Uke's trapped wrist, when combined with the attempted roll, results in breaking Uke's defensive grip so that the arm becomes released from under his body (Fig 146); indeed, it is often his stubborn refusal to participate in the roll that adds increased pressure, enabling the arm to be prised free (Fig 147).

Once the arm has come out from under Uke's body, Tori has two options: he may either attempt a Juji-gatame, where the arm is straight, or operate Ude-garami. Normally Uke will attempt to resist all efforts to straighten his arm and thus the Ude-garami is the more favoured option. Tori turns on to his side, thus exposing the freed arm, quickly switches his grip on Uke's wrist to the opposite hand and pushes his other hand through to secure a figure 4 armlock (Fig 148). From this position the Ude-garami is operated by Tori lifting Uke's forearm upwards and towards his head (Fig 149). There may be occasions when the operation of this technique results in Uke rolling over forwards in order to escape the Ude-garami. If this happens, Tori merely straightens the arm to switch back into his original intention of Juji-gatame.

Fig. 146

Fig. 147

Fig. 148

Fig. 149

VII VARIATIONS ON STRANGLES

Groundwork (Ne-waza), unlike throwing (Tachi-waza), provides many more opportunities for invention and discovery. We have found this to be the case much more with the application of strangles than other aspects of groundwork. Quite often these variations defy all attempts at finding a satisfactory Japanese name or description and can sometimes only be attributed directly to the person most notable for operating them. The following are examples of such strangles, which we have observed being used to devastating effect.

1 Yamarashi grip/Strangle variation 1 (also Adams – Great Britain)

Tori first establishes a grip with his right hand up on Uke's right lapel, ensuring that the knuckles of his fist are placed firmly against Uke's throat (Fig 150). Moving his left hand across and underneath his right hand, Tori then takes a grip fairly low down on Uke's left lapel (Fig 151). Pulling sharply across Uke's chest with the left hand and simultaneously down and across his throat with the right hand causes the strangle to come into operation (Fig 152).

This particular strangle is extremely useful for forcing a strong opponent to break his grip. Should the strangle not cause a submission, Tori may either follow through with an immediate forward throwing technique (e.g., Tai-otoshi) or take advantage of the subsequent confusion to operate a technique suitable to Uke's defensive movement.

Fig. 150

Fig. 151

Fig. 152

77

Fig. 153

Fig. 154

Fig. 155

2 Seoinage/Sode-goruma-jime

With Uke attacking with a right Seoinage, Tori first ensures that his right hand is gripping high up on Uke's left lapel and defends the technique by dropping his hips in an attempt to force Uke on to his knees (Fig 153). When he discovers that his attack has been countered, Uke will break his grip and try to adopt a defensive posture (Fig 154). Keeping his opponent firmly under control by maintaining his pull on Uke's left lapel and bearing down firmly on his back, Tori swiftly moves around the front of his opponent (Fig 155) to take up a position where his right shoulder is in contact with Uke's left shoulder blade (Fig 156). At this point Tori's right arm, which is still firmly gripping Uke's lapel, is forcing the strangle to come into operation, and Uke will more than likely attempt to roll away in order to escape the pressure. To prevent this Tori leans firmly against his opponent's left shoulder and back (Fig 157) and slips his left hand under Uke's head to take a grip on the opposite lapel, simultaneously slipping his left leg forward in order to collapse Uke on to his side so that Tori himself ends up on his back (Fig 158). Applying a firm and opposing pulling action on each lapel causes the strangle to be fully applied.

Fig. 156

Fig. 157

Fig. 158

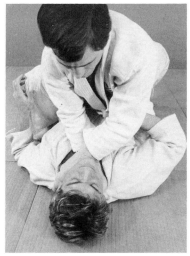

Fig. 159   Fig. 160

3 Gyaku-juji-jime (fingers in)

This particular strangle can be applied to equal effect whether Uke is attacking from on top (Fig 159) or being attacked on his back (Fig 160). Tori first establishes a normal cross-hand grip with his right hand high up on his opponent's right lapel. He then takes his left hand over his own right wrist and inserts it, fingers first, high up on Uke's collar. When he pulls his elbows downwards and towards each other, the blood supply to Uke's head is cut off and the strangle is in full operation. It should be noted that equal pressure should be applied with both arms; and when Tori is operating the technique from underneath, he should control Uke by placing him between his legs.

4 Rolling strangle (Ulch – DDR)

Approaching Uke from his left side, Tori places his right arm under Uke's throat and establishes a loose grip on his opponent's right lapel, with his fingers inside the jacket. Slipping his left hand, fingers first, under the collar at the back of Uke's neck (Fig 161), Tori drops his left elbow against the left side of his opponent's head (Fig 162) and lowers his left shoulder on to the mat, simultaneously pulling his partner towards him by tightening his grip on the jacket. By continuing to turn on to his back (Fig 163), Tori encourages Uke to roll sideways over his left shoulder and across Tori (Fig 164) – Uke generally co-operates because he sees it as his only opportunity to escape the pressure on his neck. This

Fig. 161

Fig. 162

Fig. 163

Fig. 164

Fig. 165

results in Uke lying on his back at Tori's right side (Fig 165). By throwing his left leg across Uke's body and trapping his opponent's left arm by pushing his head towards the mat, Tori can continue to operate this extremely effective strangle as well as achieving a hold-down position (Fig 166).

Fig. 166

Fig. 167

Fig. 168

5 Koshe-jime (Yamashita – Japan)

Approaching his opponent from over his left shoulder and side, Tori controls Uke by placing his right hand on the ground at a point next to and slightly inside his opponent's bent right knee (Fig 167). Maintaining firm chest contact with Uke's back, Tori places his left hand under Uke's chin and establishes a grip high up on his right lapel (Fig 168). Tori then wedges his extended right hand against the inside of Uke's right knee and side, simultaneously collapsing him into the mat by applying pressure on the head and left shoulder (Fig 169). Tori next rotates anti-clockwise and throws his right leg through in order to end up sitting just above his opponent's left shoulder (Fig 170). With Uke locked firmly into place, Tori simply leans back and pulls on his opponent's jacket in order to apply the strangle (Fig 171).

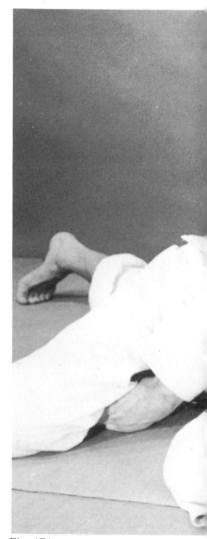

Fig. 171

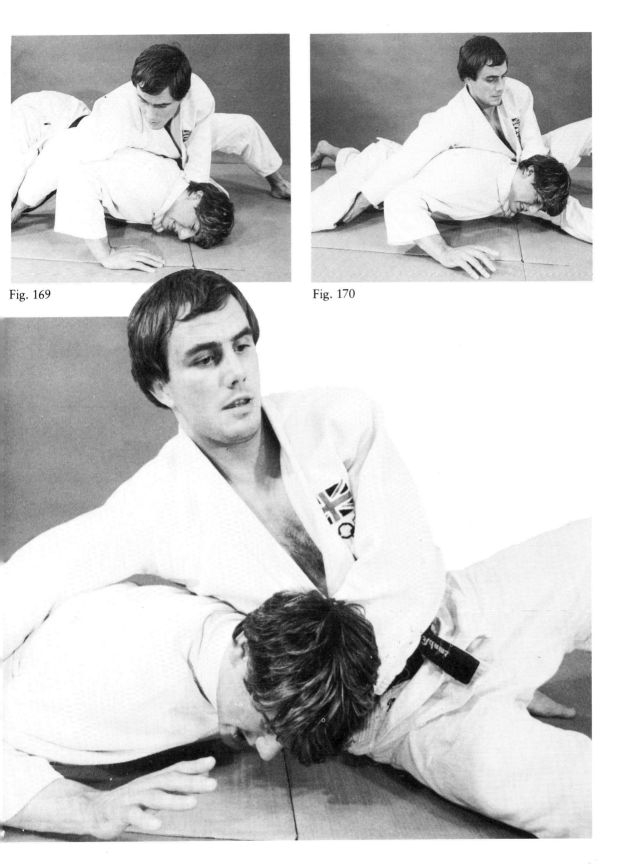

Fig. 169

Fig. 170

6 Yamarashi grip/Strangle variation 2 (Kashiwazake – Japan)

This strangle is particularly effective when swiftly pursued after an opponent has either been knocked down on to his knees or has been forced into that position in order to avoid being thrown. Tori first achieves a grip on Uke's left lapel with his left hand (Fig 172). Having initiated an attack, which results in Uke dropping down on to his knee(s), Tori swiftly steps forward to achieve close contact and reaches over his opponent's head to take a firm grip of his belt with his right hand (Fig 173). Moving to his left, Tori allows Uke to slip his head out from under his body, whereupon Tori steps forward to emphasise his hip contact against Uke's right

Fig. 173

Fig. 172

upper chest and shoulder (Fig 174) and pulls upwards with his right hand and across Uke's neck with the left hand and Uke's left collar in order to bring the strangle into operation (Fig 175). It should be noted that the same strangle can be used in a purely Ne-waza situation with Tori operating off his knees.

Fig. 174

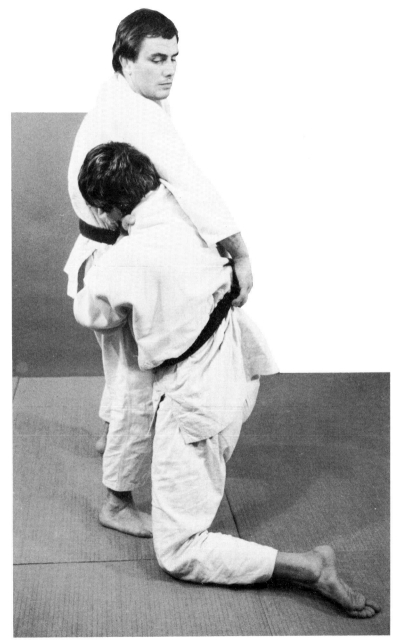

Fig. 175

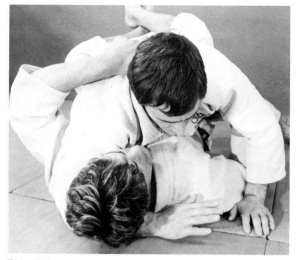
Fig. 176

Fig. 177

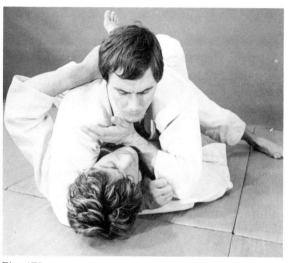
Fig. 178

Fig. 179

7 Reverse naked strangle (Neureuter – West Germany)

When Tori is attacking from above and between his
opponent's legs, he first places his right arm through and
against the back of Uke's neck (Fig 176). Bearing strongly
down on Uke's chest, Tori bends his left arm at the elbow
and takes a grip with his right hand on his own left sleeve
(Fig 177). Bringing his left forearm over to a position across
the front of Uke's throat, Tori then takes a grip, with his left
hand, on the upper part of his own right sleeve (Fig 178). The
strangle is operated when Tori pulls against his own sleeves
to exert extreme pressure with both forearms against Uke's
throat (Fig 179).

Appendix

CONTEST RULES OF THE INTERNATIONAL JUDO
FEDERATION

In this appendix we have set out to examine only those contest rules which we feel are of direct concern to the competitive player: those which affect either his ability to score or which involve the award of a penalty, thus directly affecting the possible outcome of a contest. There are many more rules set out by the International Judo Federation, the majority of which relate to custom or procedure and are therefore of more major concern to the referee or judge. That is not to say that we believe these rules should be ignored; on the contrary, they are an important part of the fabric of tradition in judo and should be understood and observed by all who practise the sport. To those who ignore, misunderstand or seek to bend the rules of contest procedure we say 'Let the player beware,' for without rules fairly and firmly applied and acknowledged all sport would degenerate to mere brawling. Always remember that the referee makes the final decision and, like it or not, this must be the strongest of all rules if any sport is to exist and flourish.

The award of Ippon (a full point) for a throwing technique is generally regarded as being applied when an opponent is thrown in such a way that both shoulder blades contact the mat simultaneously and with impetus. As a general rule of thumb this is a reasonable guide, but the player should be aware that the referee can award an Ippon score if, *in his opinion*, such a technique *merits* the score. The same provision applies to scores of Wazari (almost Ippon), Yuko (almost Wazari) and Koka (almost Yuko). The fact that a score is awarded only by the opinion of the referee (if both judges do not disagree) should lead the player to abandon his own opinions during a contest and lead him to pursue his ultimate aim: a winning score – in descending order, Ippon, two Wazaris (Wazari Awasete Ippon), Wazari, or a superior accumulation of Yukos and/or Kokas at the end of contest time. Disagreement with the referee will only affect a player's subsequent performance, and dispute – which may result in the award of a penalty – should be avoided at all costs.

The penalty of Shido (note) is generally awarded for small infringements of the rules and spirit of contest judo. These infringements normally fall into two major categories: passivity, where a competitor behaves in a manner which is designed solely to prevent his opponent from attacking; and dangerous play, where a player performs an action that could possibly lead to injury or offends the protocol (correct procedure) of a contest. A player may be awarded a Shido if he intentionally avoids taking hold of his opponent; adopts an excessively defensive posture (or no attack has taken place in general for twenty to thirty seconds after a player has already been warned); holds both of his opponent's sleeves in order to defend, or interlocks the fingers of both his own hands in order to prevent further activity. A Shido may also be awarded if a player: inserts his fingers inside an opponent's sleeve or trouser leg; winds the end of the belt or jacket around any part of the opponent's body; grips his opponent's judogi in his teeth; places an arm, foot or leg directly against an opponent's face; maintains a hold on his opponent with his legs around the neck and armpit when his opponent has succeeded in standing up or is in a position to lift him clear from the mat; takes a grip of his opponent's foot/feet, leg(s), or trouser leg(s) with the hand(s) without simultaneously operating a throwing technique. A Shido will additionally be awarded should a player at any time, intentionally and without the permission of the referee, disarrange his judogi or untie or retie his belt or trousers.

The penalty of Chui (caution) is generally awarded for medium infringements or when two successive infringements have been committed, each of which would merit an award of Shido (i.e., if a Shido penalty has already been awarded in a contest, an offence committed within the same category later in the contest will now be awarded the next highest penalty, Chui). The infringements in this category are slightly more serious in nature and are generally concerned with illegal actions which are likely to injure an opponent or gain their perpetrator an unfair advantage. A player may be awarded a Chui if he attempts to apply a leg scissors to his opponent's trunk, neck or head; if he kicks or knees the hand or arm of an opponent in order to force him to break his grip; if he attempts to place a foot or leg in the opponent's belt, collar or lapel or attempts to bend back an opponent's finger or fingers in order to force him to break his grip; for any attempt merely to pull down an opponent in order to go into groundwork; for going outside the contest area from the standing position while applying a technique started inside the contest area.

The penalty of Keikoku (warning) is generally awarded for serious infringements or in the case of a player who has already been awarded a Chui, when an offence is committed which, in itself, would merit a Shido, a Chui or a Keikoku. In the main, such infringements that would be awarded Keikoku are those which involve actions designed to injure an opponent, movements or technique which have been banned because of likelihood of causing injury, or any action which seriously contravenes the spirit of judo and the basic fabric of fair play and reasonable conduct.

A player may be awarded a Keikoku if, from a standing position, he intentionally steps outside the contest area or, with intention, forces his opponent to step outside the contest area; if he attempts to perform Kawazu-gake (winding one leg around an opponent's leg while facing, more or less, in the same direction and falling backwards on to him); if he applies a locking action against any other joint except the elbow; if he applies any action likely to cause injury to an opponent's neck or spinal vertebrae; if, having lifted an opponent from a supine position on the mat, he then forces him back on to the mat; if he attempts to sweep an opponent's leg from the inside while being attacked by a forward technique such as Harai-goshi; if he attempts to apply a technique outside the contest area; if he disregards the referee's instructions or makes unnecessary calls, remarks or gestures derogatory to the referee or opponent during the contest; if he falls directly to the ground when applying techniques such as Waki-gatame; or if he performs any other action which may injure or endanger an opponent or may be against the spirit of judo.

The most serious of offences are penalised by Hansoku-make (disqualification), which may also be awarded when continuous infringement has resulted in the award of Keikoku and a further offence is committed. Only two infringements are itemised under this offence, but it should be remembered that referees and judges are authorised to award penalties according to the 'intent' or situation and in the best interests of the sport. Hansoku-make may be awarded when a player attempts to 'dive' head first on to the mat, by bending downward and forward, while performing or attempting to perform techniques such as Uchi-mata, Hare-goshi or Harai-goshi.

It should be noted that when a Shido is awarded against one contestant, the other shall be regarded as having scored Koka; similarly a Chui is regarded as a Yuko and Keikoku as Wazari. Thus it is possible for a player to score an infinite amount of Kokas and Yukos and yet lose a contest through infringing one rule which merits the award of a higher penalty!

Although it would be impossible – possibly undesirable – to prevent players from using the rules in a tactical manner to ensure a win, there have been many occasions when such tactics have proved to be a player's downfall and, in our opinion, such play often results in negative and defensive judo – which is certainly not in the best interests, nor in the true spirit, of our sport. We did consider detailing the exact manner of each tactical ploy but decided that this might only encourage and promote such activities. Suffice it to say that these tactics generally involve 'playing the edge', defending a winning score (usually to save energy for following contests), spoiling play by operating 'collapsing' techniques, feigning injury, running time out on the ground, claiming penalties unawarded (or unwarranted), attempting to influence referees by energetic (dramatic) but totally negative play, and so on.

It is our deepest wish to see contests fought in the true spirit of judo where each player sets out to achieve the highest score by the use of positive attacking skills and 'honest' defence but, while the possibility of fame and fortune exists, we realise that this may be difficult to achieve in all cases and on all occasions. Nothing can match the feeling of standing over a difficult opponent alongside a referee holding his arm vertically aloft, knowing that your opponent's defeat is the result of time you spent practising your skills in the dojo.

Glossary

Also applicable to the Promotion Syllabi

ARASHI Storm (e.g. yama-arashi = mountain storm).
ASHI Leg, foot.
ASHIWAZA Leg/foot technique.
CHUI A caution (penalty; equivalent to 5 points).
DAN 'Leader' grade, generally black belt.
DE (v.* DERU) To come out, to advance (e.g. deashiharai).
DO (a) Way, path, etc. This word was used frequently in Chinese and Japanese philosophy in the sense of the way of doing an act in the moral and ethical sphere as well as the simple physical. Professor Kano (the founder of Judo) 'borrowed' it from these sources.
(b) Trunk of the body.
DOJO Hall or room in which Judo is practised.
ERI Collar, of a jacket.
GAKE (v. KAKERU) To hang, hook, block.
GARAMI (v. GARAMU) To entangle, wrap, bend.
GYAKU Reverse, upside down.
HA Wing.
HADAKA Naked.
HAJIME Start, referee's call to commence a contest.
HANE Spring (e.g. hanegoshi = spring hip).
HANSOKU Disqualification (penalty; equivalent to ten points).
HANTEI Judgment, the referee's call at the end of a drawn contest calling on the corner judges to indicate who in their opinion was the better of the two contestants.
HARAI (BARAI) (v. HARU) Sweep, reap.
HIDARI Left.
HIZA Knee.

* v. denotes alternative version

HON (a) Point (*see* **IPPON**), ultimate score awarded in a contest.

(b) Basic.

(c) Number suffix for counting long cylindrical objects, therefore ippon seoinage = one arm shoulder throw.

IPPON One point (score value of 10 points).

JIGOTAI Defensive posture.

JOSEKI The place in a dojo or hall where the seniors or VIPs sit.

JU (a) Soft, gentle. This word, taken from Taoist philosophy, embodies the opposite of hard, extreme, unreasonable. Hence the use of Ju in Judo does not imply soft (as a synonym of easy) but rather reasonable, efficient. Physical action in Judo is not meant to be easy (weak) so much as economic, by using the body to its best advantage, and taking active advantage of any and all weaknesses the opponent may offer, so that maximum effect can be attained with maximum efficiency.

(b) Ten.

JUDO A form of wrestling in which clothes are worn by the contestants. The clothes and belt (encircling the waist twice) allow for greater range of technique. The depth of Judo in the use of tachi-waza (techniques done in the standing position) and newaza (techniques done in the groundwork position) requires skill plus physical and mental fitness being increasingly raised to an extremely high standard. In promotion examinations (grading contests) no allowance is conceded to size or weight; success depends solely on the individual's attributes – skills, physical and mental training standards.

JUDOGI The clothes worn when practising or competing at Judo.

JUDOKA A person who practises Judo. A very senior player (at least 4th Dan).

JUJI Cross or crossing.

KAESHI (GAESHI) To counter (e.g. osotogaeshi = major outer counter).

KAESHIWAZA Counter techniques.

KAKE The point of the throw, the point of maximum power.

KAI (KWAI) Society, club.

KAKU (GAKU) An angle or corner.

KAMI (a) Upper, top.

(b) Paper.

(c) God(s).

KANSETSU A joint, articulation.

KANSETSUWAZA Technique of locking limb joints.

KATA (a) Form. A stylised set of techniques used to develop the performer's posture, balance and appreciation of the various Judo techniques.
(b) One side.
(c) Shoulder (e.g. kataguruma = shoulder wheel).

KATAME (GATAME) (v.* KATEMERU) To harden, tighten, hold (e.g. kata-gatame = shoulder hold).

KEIKOKU Warning (penalty; equivalent to 7 points).

KESA A Buddhist monk's surplice, worn diagonally across the body. Thus there is the technique known as kesagatame, which in free translation into English is referred to as 'scarf hold'.

KIAI A shout used to strengthen the body and harden the will when maximum effort is required.

KO (a) Small, minor (e.g. kouchi-gari = minor inner reaping).
(b) Old, ancient.
(c) Lecture, study, think.

KODOKAN The headquarters of Judo in Japan (Tokyo).

KOKA A score, almost a yuko (value of score, 3 points).

KOSHI (GOSHI) Hips (e.g. koshiwaza = hip techniques).

KURUMA (GURUMA) (a) Wheel (e.g. oguruma = major wheel).
(b) Vehicle.

KUZURE (v. KUZURERU) To crumble, collapse, break down. Thus a free translation of kuzurekesagatame would be 'broken scarf hold'.

KYU A judo 'student' grade.

MAKIKOMI To wrap or roll up, to throw by rolling oneself so that the opponent is whipped off his feet.

MASUTEMIWAZA Technique whereby the performer (Tori) falls straight on to his back.

MATA The inside top of the thigh.

MATTE Wait, break.

MIGI Right (as opposed to left).

MON Gate, junior grade.

MOROTE Both hands, two hands (e.g. morote-seoinage = both-hands shoulder throw).

MUNE Chest.

NAGE (v. NAGERU) To throw (e.g. nagewaza = throwing techniques).

NAGENOKATA The forms of throwing. Fifteen selected throws executed both left and right to train the participants in body control and appreciation of Judo technique.

* v. denotes alternative version

NE (v.* **NERU**) To lie down.

NEWAZA Technique done in a lying-down position.

NIGEWAZA (v. **NIGERU, NEWAZA**) Escape technique (in groundwork).

O Big, large, major (e.g. ouchigari = major inner reaping).

OKURI (v. **OKURU**) To send forward (e.g. okuri-erijime = sliding lapel neck-lock).

OSAEKOMI Holding (e.g. osaekomi-waza = holding technique(s)), referee's call signalling to the time-keeper that a hold is to be timed.

OTOSHI (v. **OTOSU**) To drop (e.g. taiotoshi = body drop).

RANDORI Free practice.

REI Bow.

RENRAKU Connection, contact.

RENRAKUWAZA Combination technique.

RENZOKUWAZA Comprehensive name for throws linked up in any way.

SASAE To support, prop (e.g. sasaitsurikomiashi = propping drawing ankle).

SEOI (v. **SEOU**) To carry on the back (e.g. seoinage).

SHIAI Contest.

SHIDO Note (penalty; equivalent to 3 points).

SHIHO Four quarters, four directions.

SHIME (**JIME**) (v. **SHIMERU**) To tighten, strangle.

SHIMEWAZA Technique of neck-locking.

SODE Sleeve.

SONOMAMA Freeze, do not move.

SORE-MADE That is all (referee's term to signify end of contest).

SOTO Outside, outer (e.g. osotogari = major outer reap).

SUKUI (v. **SUKUU**) To scoop up.

SUMI Corner.

SUTEMI (v. **SUTERU**) To throw away.

SUTEMIWAZA Technique whereby the attacker throws away his own body, sacrifices his own posture.

TACHI (v. **TATSU**) To stand.

TACHI-WAZA Technique done in the standing position.

TAI Body.

TANI Valley (e.g. taniotoshi = valley drop).

TATAMI Rice straw mats used in dojos and Japanese houses.

TATE Vertical.

TE Hand (e.g. tewaza = hand techniques).

* v. denotes alternative version

TOKETA Hold broken. A command given by a referee to indicate to the time-keeper, the contestants and the onlookers generally that a contestant has effectively broken the hold that he was being secured by.

TOMOE Turning over, twisting over, whirling over. It is difficult to find the exact translation in English, but tomoe-nage is freely translated as 'stomach throw'.

TORI (v.* TORU) (a) The name used often in technical explanation for the person who throws.
(b) To grasp, to hold in the hands.

UCHI Inside.

UCHIKOMI (v. UTSU) To beat against. A repetitive exercise where the throwing technique is taken to the point of kake.

UDE Arm.

UE Above, on top of.

UKE (v. UKERU) To take. The name used often in technical explanation for the person who is thrown.

UKEMI The 'breakfall'.

UKI (v. UKU) To float. Buoyant.

URA Back, rear, reverse.

USHIRO Behind, back of (e.g. ushirogoshi = back of hip).

UTSURI (v. UTSURU) To change, move (e.g. utsuri-goshi = changing hip).

WAKARE (v. WAKARU) To divide, separate (e.g. yokowakare = side separation).

WAZA Technique.

WAZA-ARI A score, almost an ippon (score value of 7 points).

YAMA Mountain.

YOKO Side (e.g. yokosutemiwaza = a sacrifice throw with the attacker falling on to his side in order to execute the technique).

YOSHI Carry on. A referee's instruction to a contestant to carry on with the contest.

YUKO A score, almost waza-ari (score value of 5 points).

* v. denotes alternative version